This Planner Belongs to:

_____

_____

2022

01 JANUARY

Sun	Mon	Tue	Wed	Thu	Fri	Sat
						01
02	03	04	05	06	07	08
09	10	11	12	13	14	15
16	17	18	19	20	21	22
23	24	25	26	27	28	29
30	31					

02 FEBRUARY

Sun	Mon	Tue	Wed	Thu	Fri	Sat
		01	02	03	04	05
06	07	08	09	10	11	12
13	14	15	16	17	18	19
20	21	22	23	24	25	26
27	28					

03 MARCH

Sun	Mon	Tue	Wed	Thu	Fri	Sat
		01	02	03	04	05
06	07	08	09	10	11	12
13	14	15	16	17	18	19
20	21	22	23	24	25	26
27	28	29	30	31		

04 APRIL

Sun	Mon	Tue	Wed	Thu	Fri	Sat
					01	02
03	04	05	06	07	08	09
10	11	12	13	14	15	16
17	18	19	20	21	22	23
24	25	26	27	28	29	30

05 MAY

Sun	Mon	Tue	Wed	Thu	Fri	Sat
01	02	03	04	05	06	07
08	09	10	11	12	13	14
11	01	01	01	01	01	01
15	16	17	18	19	20	21
22	23	24	25	26	27	28
29	30	31				

06 JUNE

Sun	Mon	Tue	Wed	Thu	Fri	Sat
			01	02	03	04
05	06	07	08	09	10	11
12	13	14	15	16	17	18
19	20	21	22	23	24	25
26	27	28	29	30		

07 JULY

Sun	Mon	Tue	Wed	Thu	Fri	Sat
					01	02
03	04	05	06	07	08	09
10	11	12	13	14	15	16
17	18	19	20	21	22	23
24	25	26	27	28	29	30
31						

08 AUGUST

Sun	Mon	Tue	Wed	Thu	Fri	Sat
	01	02	03	04	05	06
07	08	09	10	11	12	13
14	15	16	17	18	19	20
21	22	23	24	25	26	27
28	29	30	31			

09 SEPTEMBER

Sun	Mon	Tue	Wed	Thu	Fri	Sat
				01	02	03
04	05	06	07	08	09	10
11	12	13	14	15	16	17
18	19	20	21	22	23	24
25	26	27	28	29	30	

10 OCTOBER

Sun	Mon	Tue	Wed	Thu	Fri	Sat
						01
02	03	04	05	06	07	08
09	10	11	12	13	14	15
16	17	18	19	20	21	22
23	24	25	26	27	28	29
30	31					

11 NOVEMBER

Sun	Mon	Tue	Wed	Thu	Fri	Sat
		01	02	03	04	05
06	07	08	09	10	11	12
13	14	15	16	17	18	19
20	21	22	23	24	25	26
27	28	29	30			

12 DECEMBER

Sun	Mon	Tue	Wed	Thu	Fri	Sat
				01	02	03
04	05	06	07	08	09	10
11	12	13	14	15	16	17
18	19	20	21	22	23	24
25	26	27	28	29	30	31

Create Your January Budget Here

Monthly Incomes

#	Source	Amount	Date
1			
2			
3			
4			
5			

Total Income: _____

Monthly Expenses

Healthcare

Health Insurance	
Life Insurance	
Dental Insurance	
Doctor Appointment(S)	
Optometry Appointment(S)	
Dental Appointment(S)	
Prescriptions	
Other Medical Expenses	

Total Healthcare: _____

Monthly Expenses (utilities)

Rent/Mortgage	
Electricity Bill	
Water Bill	
Sewage/Trash	
Cabel Bill	
Internet	
Phone Bill(S)	

Total Utilites: _____

notes

Living Expenses

Groceries	
Beauty Suplies	
Beauty Appointments	
Membership Dues/Fees	
Daycare/Babysitter	
School Supplies	
School Club(S) Due/Fees	
New Clothing	
Allowances	
Other Living Expenses	

Total Lilving Expenses: _____

January _____

Monthly Expenses

Pet Expenses

Pet Expenses	
Pet Food	
Veterinary Appointments	
New Toys / Treats	
Pet Sitter / Daycare	
Other Pet Expenses	

Total Pet Expenses:

Monthly Expenses

Housing Expenses

Renter's / Homeowner's Insurance	
Cleaning Supplies	
Gardening Supplies	
Furnishings	
Laundry / Dry Cleaning	
Home Maintenance / Repairs	
Household Necessities	
Other Housing Expenses	

Total Housing Expenses:

Transportation

Automobile Insurance	
Automobile Payments	
Monthly Fuel Costs	
Repairs / Maintenance	
Fares / Tickets / Etc	
Other Transportation Expenses	

Total Transportation: _____

Recreation

Vacation	
Dining Out	
Entertainment	
Social Events	
Other Recreation Expenses	

Total Recreation Expenses:

Gift Expenses

Monthly Birthdays	
Monthly Holidays	
Other Gift Expenses	

Total Gift Expenses: _____

Savings

Emergency Fund	
Education Fund	
Retirement Fund	

Total Savings: _____

January _____

Monthly Expenses

Devts

Credit Card #1	
Credit Card #2	
Credit Card #2	
Credit Card #3	
Credit Card #4	
Private Debts	
Other Debts	

Total Debts: _____

Other Expenses

Other Expenses #1	
Other Expenses #2	
Other Expenses #3	
Other Expenses #4	
Other Expenses #5	
Other Expenses #6	

Total Other Expenses: _____

Monthly Budget

Total Income	
-Total Expenses	

Mothly Remaining: _____

Monthly Notes

Monthly Bill Tracking

Paid	Bill Name	Due Date	Amount Due	Amount Paid	Balance	Payment Method / Notes

$ Create Your February Budget Here $

Monthly Incomes

#	Source	Amount	Date
1			
2			
3			
4			
5			

Total Income:_____

Monthly Expenses

Healthcare

Health Insurance	
Life Insurance	
Dental Insurance	
Doctor Appointment(S)	
Optometry Appointment(S)	
Dental Appointment(S)	
Prescriptions	
Other Medical Expenses	

Total Healthcare:_____

Monthly Expenses (utilities)

Rent/Mortgage	
Electricity Bill	
Water Bill	
Sewage/Trash	
Cabel Bill	
Internet	
Phone Bill(S)	

Total Utilites:_____

notes

Living Expenses

Groceries	
Beauty Suplies	
Beauty Appointments	
Membership Dues/Fees	
Daycare/Babysitter	
School Supplies	
School Club(S) Due/Fees	
New Clothing	
Allowances	
Other Living Expenses	

Total Lilving Expenses:_____

February _____

Monthly Expenses

Pet Expenses

Pet Expenses	
Pet Food	
Veterinary Appointments	
New Toys / Treats	
Pet Sitter / Daycare	
Other Pet Expenses	

Total Pet Expenses:

Transportation

Automobile Insurance	
Automobile Payments	
Monthly Fuel Costs	
Repairs / Maintenance	
Fares / Tickets / Etc	
Other Transportation Expenses	

Total Transportation:_____

Gift Expenses

Monthly Birthdays	
Monthly Holidays	
Other Gift Expenses	

Total Gift Expenses:_____

Monthly Expenses

Housing Expenses

Renter's / Homeowner's Insurance	
Cleaning Supplies	
Gradening Supplies	
Furnishings	
Laundry / Dry Cleaning	
Home Maintenance / Repairs	
Household Necessities	
Other Housing Expenses	

Total Housing Expenses:

Recreation

Vacation	
Dining Out	
Entertainment	
Social Events	
Other Recreation Expenses	

Total Recreation Expenses:

Savings

Emergency Fund	
Education Fund	
Retirement Fund	

Total Savings: _____

February _____

Monthly Expenses

Devts

Credit Card #1	
Credit Card #2	
Credit Card #2	
Credit Card #3	
Credit Card #4	
Private Debts	
Other Debts	

Total Debts: _____

Other Expenses

Other Expenses #1	
Other Expenses #2	
Other Expenses #3	
Other Expenses #4	
Other Expenses #5	
Other Expenses #6	

Total Other Expenses: _____

Monthly Budget

Total Income	
-Total Expenses	

Mothly Remaining: _____

Monthly Notes

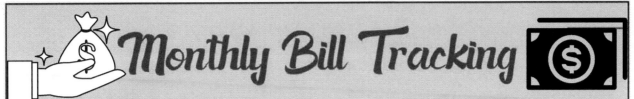

Monthly Bill Tracking

Paid	Bill Name	Due Date	Amount Due	Amount Paid	Balance	Payment Method / Notes

Create Your March Budget Here

Monthly Incomes

#	Source	Amount	Date
1			
2			
3			
4			
5			

Total Income:_____

Monthly Expenses

Healthcare

Health Insurance	
Life Insurance	
Dental Insurance	
Doctor Appointment(S)	
Optometry Appointment(S)	
Dental Appointment(S)	
Prescriptions	
Other Medical Expenses	

Total Healthcare:_____

Monthly Expenses (utilities)

Rent/Mortgage	
Electricity Bill	
Water Bill	
Sewage/Trash	
Cabel Bill	
Internet	
Phone Bill(S)	

Total Utilites:_____

notes

Living Expenses

Groceries	
Beauty Suplies	
Beauty Appointments	
Membership Dues/Fees	
Daycare/Babysitter	
School Supplies	
School Club(S) Due/Fees	
New Clothing	
Allowances	
Other Living Expenses	

Total Lilving Expenses:_____

March _____

Monthly Expenses

Pet Expenses

Pet Expenses	
Pet Food	
Veterinary Appointments	
New Toys / Treats	
Pet Sitter / Daycare	
Other Pet Expenses	

Total Pet Expenses:

Transportation

Automobile Insurance	
Automobile Payments	
Monthly Fuel Costs	
Repairs / Maintenance	
Fares / Tickets / Etc	
Other Transportation Expenses	

Total Transportation: _____

Gift Expenses

Monthly Birthdays	
Monthly Holidays	
Other Gift Expenses	

Total Gift Expenses: _____

Monthly Expenses

Housing Expenses

Renter's / Homeowner's Insurance	
Cleaning Supplies	
Gradening Supplies	
Furnishings	
Laundry / Dry Cleaning	
Home Maintenance / Repairs	
Household Necessities	
Other Housing Expenses	

Total Housing Expenses:

Recreation

Vacation	
Dining Out	
Entertainment	
Social Events	
Other Recreation Expenses	

Total Recreation Expenses:

Savings

Emergency Fund	
Education Fund	
Retirement Fund	

Total Savings: _____

March _____

Monthly Expenses

Monthly Notes

Devts

Credit Card #1	
Credit Card #2	
Credit Card #2	
Credit Card #3	
Credit Card #4	
Private Debts	
Other Debts	

Total Debts: _____

Other Expenses

Other Expenses #1	
Other Expenses #2	
Other Expenses #3	
Other Expenses #4	
Other Expenses #5	
Other Expenses #6	

Total Other Expenses: _____

Monthly Budget

Total Income	
-Total Expenses	

Mothly Remaining: _____

Monthly Bill Tracking

Paid	Bill Name	Due Date	Amount Due	Amount Paid	Balance	Payment Method / Notes

Create Your April Budget Here

Monthly Incomes

#	Source	Amount	Date
1			
2			
3			
4			
5			

Total Income: _____

Monthly Expenses

Healthcare

Health Insurance	
Life Insurance	
Dental Insurance	
Doctor Appointment(S)	
Optometry Appointment(S)	
Dental Appointment(S)	
Prescriptions	
Other Medical Expenses	

Total Healthcare: _____

Monthly Expenses (utilities)

Rent/Mortgage	
Electricity Bill	
Water Bill	
Sewage/Trash	
Cabel Bill	
Internet	
Phone Bill(S)	

Total Utilites: _____

notes

Living Expenses

Groceries
Beauty Suplies
Beauty Appointments
Membership Dues/Fees
Daycare/Babysitter
School Supplies
School Club(S) Due/Fees
New Clothing
Allowances
Other Living Expenses

Total Lilving Expenses: _____

April _____

Monthly Expenses

Pet Expenses

Pet Expenses	
Pet Food	
Veterinary Appointments	
New Toys / Treats	
Pet Sitter / Daycare	
Other Pet Expenses	

Total Pet Expenses:

Transportation

Automobile Insurance	
Automobile Payments	
Monthly Fuel Costs	
Repairs / Maintenance	
Fares / Tickets / Etc	
Other Transportation Expenses	

Total Transportation:_____

Gift Expenses

Monthly Birthdays	
Monthly Holidays	
Other Gift Expenses	

Total Gift Expenses:_____

Monthly Expenses

Housing Expenses

Renter's / Homeowner's Insurance	
Cleaning Supplies	
Gradening Supplies	
Furnishings	
Laundry / Dry Cleaning	
Home Maintenance / Repairs	
Household Necessities	
Other Housing Expenses	

Total Housing Expenses:

Recreation

Vacation	
Dining Out	
Entertainment	
Social Events	
Other Recreation Expenses	

Total Recreation Expenses:

Savings

Emergency Fund	
Education Fund	
Retirement Fund	

Total Savings:_____

April _____

Monthly Expenses

Devts

Credit Card #1	
Credit Card #2	
Credit Card #2	
Credit Card #3	
Credit Card #4	
Private Debts	
Other Debts	

Total Debts: _____

Other Expenses

Other Expenses #1	
Other Expenses #2	
Other Expenses #3	
Other Expenses #4	
Other Expenses #5	
Other Expenses #6	

Total Other Expenses: _____

Monthly Budget

Total Income	
-Total Expenses	

Mothly Remaining: _____

Monthly Notes

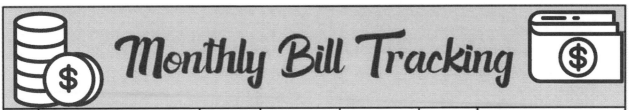

Monthly Bill Tracking

Paid	Bill Name	Due Date	Amount Due	Amount Paid	Balance	Payment Method / Notes

Create Your May Budget Here

Monthly Incomes

#	Source	Amount	Date
1			
2			
3			
4			
5			

Total Income: _____

Monthly Expenses

Healthcare

Health Insurance	
Life Insurance	
Dental Insurance	
Doctor Appointment(S)	
Optometry Appointment(S)	
Dental Appointment(S)	
Prescriptions	
Other Medical Expenses	

Total Healthcare: _____

Monthly Expenses (utilities)

Rent/Mortgage	
Electricity Bill	
Water Bill	
Sewage/Trash	
Cabel Bill	
Internet	
Phone Bill(S)	

Total Utilites: _____

notes

Living Expenses

Groceries	
Beauty Suplies	
Beauty Appointments	
Membership Dues/Fees	
Daycare/Babysitter	
School Supplies	
School Club(S) Due/Fees	
New Clothing	
Allowances	
Other Living Expenses	

Total Lilving Expenses: _____

May _____

Monthly Expenses

Pet Expenses

Pet Expenses	
Pet Food	
Veterinary Appointments	
New Toys / Treats	
Pet Sitter / Daycare	
Other Pet Expenses	

Total Pet Expenses:

Transportation

Automobile Insurance	
Automobile Payments	
Monthly Fuel Costs	
Repairs / Maintenance	
Fares / Tickets / Etc	
Other Transportation Expenses	

Total Transportation: _____

Gift Expenses

Monthly Birthdays	
Monthly Holidays	
Other Gift Expenses	

Total Gift Expenses: _____

Monthly Expenses

Housing Expenses

Renter's / Homeowner's Insurance	
Cleaning Supplies	
Gardening Supplies	
Furnishings	
Laundry / Dry Cleaning	
Home Maintenance / Repairs	
Household Necessities	
Other Housing Expenses	

Total Housing Expenses:

Recreation

Vacation	
Dining Out	
Entertainment	
Social Events	
Other Recreation Expenses	

Total Recreation Expenses:

Savings

Emergency Fund	
Education Fund	
Retirement Fund	

Total Savings: _____

$

May _____

Monthly Expenses

Devts

Credit Card #1	
Credit Card #2	
Credit Card #2	
Credit Card #3	
Credit Card #4	
Private Debts	
Other Debts	

Total Debts: _____

Other Expenses

Other Expenses #1	
Other Expenses #2	
Other Expenses #3	
Other Expenses #4	
Other Expenses #5	
Other Expenses #6	

Total Other Expenses: _____

Monthly Budget

Total Income	
-Total Expenses	

Mothly Remaining: _____

Monthly Notes

Monthly Bill Tracking

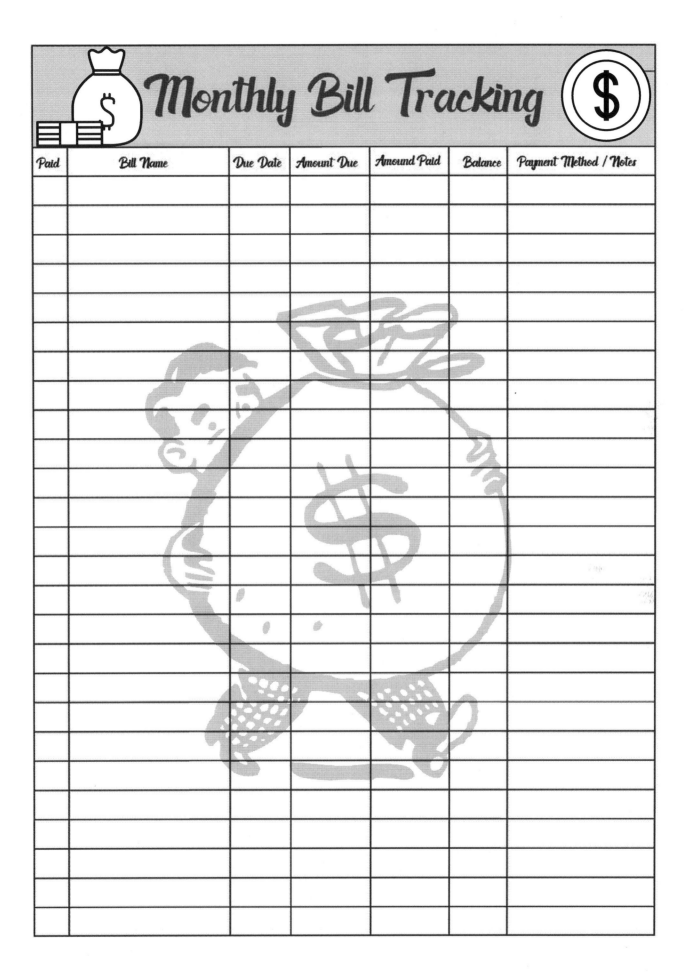

Paid	Bill Name	Due Date	Amount Due	Amount Paid	Balance	Payment Method / Notes

Create Your June Budget Here

Monthly Incomes

#	Source	Amount	Date
1			
2			
3			
4			
5			

Total Income:_____

Monthly Expenses

Healthcare

Health Insurance	
Life Insurance	
Dental Insurance	
Doctor Appointment(S)	
Optometry Appointment(S)	
Dental Appointment(S)	
Prescriptions	
Other Medical Expenses	

Total Healthcare:_____

Monthly Expenses (utilities)

Rent/Mortgage	
Electricity Bill	
Water Bill	
Sewage/Trash	
Cabel Bill	
Internet	
Phone Bill(S)	

Total Utilites:_____

notes

Living Expenses

Groceries
Beauty Suplies
Beauty Appointments
Membership Dues/Fees
Daycare/Babysitter
School Supplies
School Club(S) Due/Fees
New Clothing
Allowances
Other Living Expenses

Total Lilving Expenses:_____

June _____

Monthly Expenses

Pet Expenses

Pet Expenses	
Pet Food	
Veterinary Appointments	
New Toys / Treats	
Pet Sitter / Daycare	
Other Pet Expenses	

Total Pet Expenses:

Transportation

Automobile Insurance	
Automobile Payments	
Monthly Fuel Costs	
Repairs / Maintenance	
Fares / Tickets / Etc	
Other Transportation Expenses	

Total Transportation: _____

Gift Expenses

Monthly Birthdays	
Monthly Holidays	
Other Gift Expenses	

Total Gift Expenses: _____

Monthly Expenses

Housing Expenses

Renter's / Homeowner's Insurance	
Cleaning Supplies	
Gardening Supplies	
Furnishings	
Laundry / Dry Cleaning	
Home Maintenance / Repairs	
Household Necessities	
Other Housing Expenses	

Total Housing Expenses:

Recreation

Vacation	
Dining Out	
Entertainment	
Social Events	
Other Recreation Expenses	

Total Recreation Expenses:

Savings

Emergency Fund	
Education Fund	
Retirement Fund	

Total Savings: _____

June _____

Monthly Expenses

Devts

Credit Card #1	
Credit Card #2	
Credit Card #2	
Credit Card #3	
Credit Card #4	
Private Debts	
Other Debts	

Total Debts: _____

Other Expenses

Other Expenses #1	
Other Expenses #2	
Other Expenses #3	
Other Expenses #4	
Other Expenses #5	
Other Expenses #6	

Total Other Expenses: _____

Monthly Budget

Total Income	
-Total Expenses	

Mothly Remaining: _____

Monthly Notes

Monthly Bill Tracking

Paid	Bill Name	Due Date	Amount Due	Amound Paid	Balance	Payment Method / Notes

Create Your July Budget Here

Monthly Incomes

#	Source	Amount	Date
1			
2			
3			
4			
5			

Total Income:_____

Monthly Expenses

Healthcare

Health Insurance	
Life Insurance	
Dental Insurance	
Doctor Appointment(S)	
Optometry Appointment(S)	
Dental Appointment(S)	
Prescriptions	
Other Medical Expenses	

Total Healthcare:_____

Monthly Expenses (utilities)

Rent/Mortgage	
Electricity Bill	
Water Bill	
Sewage/Trash	
Cabel Bill	
Internet	
Phone Bill(S)	

Total Utilites:_____

notes

Living Expenses

Groceries
Beauty Suplies
Beauty Appointments
Membership Dues/Fees
Daycare/Babysitter
School Supplies
School Club(S) Due/Fees
New Clothing
Allowances
Other Living Expenses

Total Lilving Expenses:_____

July _____

Monthly Expenses

Pet Expenses

Pet Expenses	
Pet Food	
Veterinary Appointments	
New Toys / Treats	
Pet Sitter / Daycare	
Other Pet Expenses	

Total Pet Expenses:

Transportation

Automobile Insurance	
Automobile Payments	
Monthly Fuel Costs	
Repairs / Maintenance	
Fares / Tickets / Etc	
Other Transportation Expenses	

Total Transportation: _____

Gift Expenses

Monthly Birthdays	
Monthly Holidays	
Other Gift Expenses	

Total Gift Expenses: _____

Monthly Expenses

Housing Expenses

Renter's / Homeowner's Insurance	
Cleaning Supplies	
Gradening Supplies	
Furnishings	
Laundry / Dry Cleaning	
Home Maintenance / Repairs	
Household Necessities	
Other Housing Expenses	

Total Housing Expenses:

Recreation

Vacation	
Dining Out	
Entertainment	
Social Events	
Other Recreation Expenses	

Total Recreation Expenses:

Savings

Emergency Fund	
Education Fund	
Retirement Fund	

Total Savings: _____

July _____

Monthly Expenses

Devts

Credit Card #1	
Credit Card #2	
Credit Card #2	
Credit Card #3	
Credit Card #4	
Private Debts	
Other Debts	

Total Debts: _____

Other Expenses

Other Expenses #1	
Other Expenses #2	
Other Expenses #3	
Other Expenses #4	
Other Expenses #5	
Other Expenses #6	

Total Other Expenses: _____

Monthly Budget

Total Income	
- Total Expenses	

Mothly Remaining: _____

Monthly Notes

Monthly Bill Tracking

Paid	Bill Name	Due Date	Amount Due	Amound Paid	Balance	Payment Method / Notes

%✓ Create Your August Budget Here %✓

Monthly Incomes

#	Source	Amount	Date
1			
2			
3			
4			
5			

Total Income: _____

Monthly Expenses

Healthcare

Health Insurance	
Life Insurance	
Dental Insurance	
Doctor Appointment(S)	
Optometry Appointment(S)	
Dental Appointment(S)	
Prescriptions	
Other Medical Expenses	

Total Healthcare: _____

Monthly Expenses (utilities)

Rent/Mortgage	
Electricity Bill	
Water Bill	
Sewage/Trash	
Cabel Bill	
Internet	
Phone Bill(S)	

Total Utilites: _____

notes

_____
_____
_____
_____

Living Expenses

Groceries	
Beauty Suplies	
Beauty Appointments	
Membership Dues/Fees	
Daycare/Babysitter	
School Supplies	
School Club(S) Due/Fees	
New Clothing	
Allowances	
Other Living Expenses	

Total Lilving Expenses: _____

August _____

Monthly Expenses

Pet Expenses

Pet Expenses	
Pet Food	
Veterinary Appointments	
New Toys / Treats	
Pet Sitter / Daycare	
Other Pet Expenses	

Total Pet Expenses:

Transportation

Automobile Insurance	
Automobile Payments	
Monthly Fuel Costs	
Repairs / Maintenance	
Fares / Tickets / Etc	
Other Transportation Expenses	

Total Transportation:_____

Gift Expenses

Monthly Birthdays	
Monthly Holidays	
Other Gift Expenses	

Total Gift Expenses:_____

Monthly Expenses

Housing Expenses

Renter's / Homeowner's Insurance	
Cleaning Supplies	
Gradening Supplies	
Furnishings	
Laundry / Dry Cleaning	
Home Maintenance / Repairs	
Household Necessities	
Other Housing Expenses	

Total Housing Expenses:

Recreation

Vacation	
Dining Out	
Entertainment	
Social Events	
Other Recreation Expenses	

Total Recreation Expenses:

Savings

Emergency Fund	
Education Fund	
Retirement Fund	

Total Savings:_____

August _____

Monthly Expenses

Devts

Credit Card #1	
Credit Card #2	
Credit Card #2	
Credit Card #3	
Credit Card #4	
Private Debts	
Other Debts	

Total Debts: _____

Other Expenses

Other Expenses #1	
Other Expenses #2	
Other Expenses #3	
Other Expenses #4	
Other Expenses #5	
Other Expenses #6	

Total Other Expenses: _____

Monthly Budget

Total Income	
-Total Expenses	

Mothly Remaining: _____

Monthly Notes

Monthly Bill Tracking

Paid	Bill Name	Due Date	Amount Due	Amount Paid	Balance	Payment Method / Notes

Create Your September Budget Here

Monthly Incomes

#	Source	Amount	Date
1			
2			
3			
4			
5			

Total Income:_____

Monthly Expenses

Healthcare

Health Insurance	
Life Insurance	
Dental Insurance	
Doctor Appointment(S)	
Optometry Appointment(S)	
Dental Appointment(S)	
Prescriptions	
Other Medical Expenses	

Total Healthcare:_____

Monthly Expenses (utilities)

Rent/Mortgage	
Electricity Bill	
Water Bill	
Sewage/Trash	
Cabel Bill	
Internet	
Phone Bill(S)	

Total Utilites:_____

notes

Living Expenses

Groceries
Beauty Suplies
Beauty Appointments
Membership Dues/Fees
Daycare/Babysitter
School Supplies
School Club(S) Due/Fees
New Clothing
Allowances
Other Living Expenses

Total Lilving Expenses:_____

September

Monthly Expenses

Pet Expenses

Pet Expenses	
Pet Food	
Veterinary Appointments	
New Toys / Treats	
Pet Sitter / Daycare	
Other Pet Expenses	

Total Pet Expenses:

Transportation

Automobile Insurance	
Automobile Payments	
Monthly Fuel Costs	
Repairs / Maintenance	
Fares / Tickets / Etc	
Other Transportarion Expenses	

Total Transportation:_____

Gift Expenses

Monthly Birthdays	
Monthly Holidays	
Other Gift Expenses	

Total Gift Expenses:_____

Monthly Expenses

Housing Expenses

Renter's / Homeowner's Insurance	
Cleaning Supplies	
Gradening Supplies	
Furnishings	
Laundry / Dry Cleaning	
Home Maintenance / Repairs	
Household Necessities	
Other Housing Expenses	

Total Housing Expenses:

Recreation

Vacation	
Dining Out	
Entertainment	
Social Events	
Other Recreation Expenses	

Total Recreation Expenses:

Savings

Emergency Fund	
Education Fund	
Retirement Fund	

Total Savings:_____

September

Monthly Expenses

Devts

Credit Card #1	
Credit Card #2	
Credit Card #2	
Credit Card #3	
Credit Card #4	
Private Debts	
Other Debts	

Total Debts: _____

Other Expenses

Other Expenses #1	
Other Expenses #2	
Other Expenses #3	
Other Expenses #4	
Other Expenses #5	
Other Expenses #6	

Total Other Expenses: _____

Monthly Budget

Total Income	
-Total Expenses	

Mothly Remaining: _____

Monthly Notes

Monthly Bill Tracking

Paid	Bill Name	Due Date	Amount Due	Amount Paid	Balance	Payment Method / Notes

Create Your October Budget Here

Monthly Incomes

#	Source	Amount	Date
1			
2			
3			
4			
5			

Total Income:_____

Monthly Expenses

Healthcare

Health Insurance	
Life Insurance	
Dental Insurance	
Doctor Appointment(S)	
Optometry Appointment(S)	
Dental Appointment(S)	
Prescriptions	
Other Medical Expenses	

Total Healthcare:_____

Monthly Expenses (utilities)

Rent/Mortgage	
Electricity Bill	
Water Bill	
Sewage/Trash	
Cabel Bill	
Internet	
Phone Bill(S)	

Total Utilites:_____

notes

Living Expenses

Groceries
Beauty Suplies
Beauty Appointments
Membership Dues/Fees
Daycare/Babysitter
School Supplies
School Club(S) Due/Fees
New Clothing
Allowances
Other Living Expenses

Total Lilving Expenses:_____

October _____

Monthly Expenses

Pet Expenses

Pet Expenses	
Pet Food	
Veterinary Appointments	
New Toys / Treats	
Pet Sitter / Daycare	
Other Pet Expenses	

Total Pet Expenses:

Monthly Expenses

Housing Expenses

Renter's / Homeowner's Insurance	
Cleaning Supplies	
Gradening Supplies	
Furnishings	
Laundry / Dry Cleaning	
Home Maintenance / Repairs	
Household Necessities	
Other Housing Expenses	

Total Housing Expenses:

Transportation

Automobile Insurance	
Automobile Payments	
Monthly Fuel Costs	
Repairs / Maintenance	
Fares / Tickets / Etc	
Other Transportation Expenses	

Total Transportation: _____

Recreation

Vacation	
Dining Out	
Entertainment	
Social Events	
Other Recreation Expenses	

Total Recreation Expenses:

Gift Expenses

Monthly Birthdays	
Monthly Holidays	
Other Gift Expenses	

Total Gift Expenses: _____

Savings

Emergency Fund	
Education Fund	
Retirement Fund	

Total Savings: _____

$ € £   October_____

Monthly Expenses

Devts

Credit Card #1	
Credit Card #2	
Credit Card #2	
Credit Card #3	
Credit Card #4	
Private Debts	
Other Debts	

Total Debts:_____

Other Expenses

Other Expenses #1	
Other Expenses #2	
Other Expenses #3	
Other Expenses #4	
Other Expenses #5	
Other Expenses #6	

Total Other Expenses:_____

Monthly Budget

Total Income	
-Total Expenses	

Mothly Remaining:_____

Monthly Notes

Monthly Bill Tracking

Paid	Bill Name	Due Date	Amount Due	Amound Paid	Balance	Payment Method / Notes

Create Your November Budget Here

Monthly Incomes

#	Source	Amount	Date
1			
2			
3			
4			
5			

Total Income: _____

Monthly Expenses

Healthcare

Health Insurance	
Life Insurance	
Dental Insurance	
Doctor Appointment(S)	
Optometry Appointment(S)	
Dental Appointment(S)	
Prescriptions	
Other Medical Expenses	

Total Healthcare: _____

Monthly Expenses (utilities)

Rent/Mortgage	
Electricity Bill	
Water Bill	
Sewage/Trash	
Cabel Bill	
Internet	
Phone Bill(S)	

Total Utilites: _____

notes

Living Expenses

Groceries
Beauty Suplies
Beauty Appointments
Membership Dues/Fees
Daycare/Babysitter
School Supplies
School Club(S) Due/Fees
New Clothing
Allowances
Other Living Expenses

Total Lilving Expenses: _____

Novemver_____

Monthly Expenses

Pet Expenses

Pet Expenses	
Pet Food	
Veterinary Appointments	
New Toys / Treats	
Pet Sitter / Daycare	
Other Pet Expenses	

Total Pet Expenses:

Transportation

Automobile Insurance	
Automobile Payments	
Monthly Fuel Costs	
Repairs / Maintenance	
Fares / Tickets / Etc	
Other Transportation Expenses	

Total Transportation:_____

Gift Expenses

Monthly Birthdays	
Monthly Holidays	
Other Gift Expenses	

Total Gift Expenses:_____

Monthly Expenses

Housing Expenses

Renter's / Homeowner's Insurance	
Cleaning Supplies	
Gradening Supplies	
Furnishings	
Laundry / Dry Cleaning	
Home Maintenance / Repairs	
Household Necessities	
Other Housing Expenses	

Total Housing Expenses:

Recreation

Vacation	
Dining Out	
Entertainment	
Social Events	
Other Recreation Expenses	

Total Recreation Expenses:

Savings

Emergency Fund	
Education Fund	
Retirement Fund	

Total Savings:_____

Novemver

Monthly Expenses

Devts

Credit Card #1	
Credit Card #2	
Credit Card #2	
Credit Card #3	
Credit Card #4	
Private Debts	
Other Debts	

Total Debts: _____

Other Expenses

Other Expenses #1	
Other Expenses #2	
Other Expenses #3	
Other Expenses #4	
Other Expenses #5	
Other Expenses #6	

Total Other Expenses: _____

Monthly Budget

Total Income	
-Total Expenses	

Mothly Remaining: _____

Monthly Notes

 Monthly Bill Tracking

Paid	Bill Name	Due Date	Amount Due	Amount Paid	Balance	Payment Method / Notes

Create Your December Budget Here

Monthly Incomes

#	Source	Amount	Date
1			
2			
3			
4			
5			

Total Income: _____

Monthly Expenses

Healthcare

Health Insurance	
Life Insurance	
Dental Insurance	
Doctor Appointment(S)	
Optometry Appointment(S)	
Dental Appointment(S)	
Prescriptions	
Other Medical Expenses	

Total Healthcare: _____

Monthly Expenses (utilities)

Rent/Mortgage	
Electricity Bill	
Water Bill	
Sewage/Trash	
Cabel Bill	
Internet	
Phone Bill(S)	

Total Utilites: _____

notes

Living Expenses

Groceries
Beauty Suplies
Beauty Appointments
Membership Dues/Fees
Daycare/Babysitter
School Supplies
School Club(S) Due/Fees
New Clothing
Allowances
Other Living Expenses

Total Lilving Expenses: _____

December_____

Monthly Expenses

Pet Expenses

Pet Expenses	
Pet Food	
Veterinary Appointments	
New Toys / Treats	
Pet Sitter / Daycare	
Other Pet Expenses	

Total Pet Expenses:

Transportation

Automobile Insurance	
Automobile Payments	
Monthly Fuel Costs	
Repairs / Maintenance	
Fares / Tickets / Etc	
Other Transportation Expenses	

Total Transportation:_____

Gift Expenses

Monthly Birthdays	
Monthly Holidays	
Other Gift Expenses	

Total Gift Expenses:_____

Monthly Expenses

Housing Expenses

Renter's / Homeowner's Insurance	
Cleaning Supplies	
Gradening Supplies	
Furnishings	
Laundry / Dry Cleaning	
Home Maintenance / Repairs	
Household Necessities	
Other Housing Expenses	

Total Housing Expenses:

Recreation

Vacation	
Dining Out	
Entertainment	
Social Events	
Other Recreation Expenses	

Total Recreation Expenses:

Savings

Emergency Fund	
Education Fund	
Retirement Fund	

Total Savings:_____

December _____

Monthly Expenses

Devts

Credit Card #1	
Credit Card #2	
Credit Card #2	
Credit Card #3	
Credit Card #4	
Private Debts	
Other Debts	

Total Debts: _____

Other Expenses

Other Expenses #1	
Other Expenses #2	
Other Expenses #3	
Other Expenses #4	
Other Expenses #5	
Other Expenses #6	

Total Other Expenses: _____

Monthly Budget

Total Income	
-Total Expenses	

Mothly Remaining: _____

Monthly Notes

Monthly Bill Tracking

Paid	Bill Name	Due Date	Amount Due	Amound Paid	Balance	Payment Method / Notes

Create Your January Budget Here

Monthly Incomes

#	Source	Amount	Date
1			
2			
3			
4			
5			

Total Income: _____

Monthly Expenses

Healthcare

Health Insurance	
Life Insurance	
Dental Insurance	
Doctor Appointment(S)	
Optometry Appointment(S)	
Dental Appointment(S)	
Prescriptions	
Other Medical Expenses	

Total Healthcare: _____

Monthly Expenses (utilities)

Rent/Mortgage	
Electricity Bill	
Water Bill	
Sewage/Trash	
Cabel Bill	
Internet	
Phone Bill(S)	

Total Utilites: _____

notes

Living Expenses

Groceries	
Beauty Suplies	
Beauty Appointments	
Membership Dues/Fees	
Daycare/Babysitter	
School Supplies	
School Club(S) Due/Fees	
New Clothing	
Allowances	
Other Living Expenses	

Total Lilving Expenses:

January _____

Monthly Expenses
Pet Expenses _____

Pet Expenses	
Pet Food	
Veterinary Appointments	
New Toys / Treats	
Pet Sitter / Daycare	
Other Pet Expenses	

Total Pet Expenses:

Monthly Expenses
Housing Expenses _____

Renter's / Homeowner's Insurance	
Cleaning Supplies	
Gradening Supplies	
Furnishings	
Laundry / Dry Cleaning	
Home Maintenance / Repairs	
Household Necessities	
Other Housing Expenses	

Total Housing Expenses:

Transportation

Automobile Insurance	
Automobile Payments	
Monthly Fuel Costs	
Repairs / Maintenance	
Fares / Tickets / Etc	
Other Transportation Expenses	

Total Transportation:_____

Recreation

Vacation	
Dining Out	
Entertainment	
Social Events	
Other Recreation Expenses	

Total Recreation Expenses:

Gift Expenses

Monthly Birthdays	
Monthly Holidays	
Other Gift Expenses	

Total Gift Expenses:_____

Savings

Emergency Fund	
Education Fund	
Retirement Fund	

Total Savings:_____

January _____

Monthly Expenses

Devts

Credit Card #1	
Credit Card #2	
Credit Card #2	
Credit Card #3	
Credit Card #4	
Private Debts	
Other Debts	

Total Debts: _____

Other Expenses

Other Expenses #1	
Other Expenses #2	
Other Expenses #3	
Other Expenses #4	
Other Expenses #5	
Other Expenses #6	

Total Other Expenses: _____

Monthly Budget

Total Income	
-Total Expenses	

Mothly Remaining: _____

Monthly Notes

Monthly Bill Tracking

Paid	Bill Name	Due Date	Amount Due	Amount Paid	Balance	Payment Method / Notes

$ Create Your February Budget Here $

Monthly Incomes

#	Source	Amount	Date
1			
2			
3			
4			
5			

Total Income:_____

Monthly Expenses

Healthcare

Health Insurance	
Life Insurance	
Dental Insurance	
Doctor Appointment(S)	
Optometry Appointment(S)	
Dental Appointment(S)	
Prescriptions	
Other Medical Expenses	

Total Healthcare:_____

Monthly Expenses (utilities)

Rent/Mortgage	
Electricity Bill	
Water Bill	
Sewage/Trash	
Cabel Bill	
Internet	
Phone Bill(S)	

Total Utilites:_____

notes

Living Expenses

Groceries	
Beauty Suplies	
Beauty Appointments	
Membership Dues/Fees	
Daycare/Babysitter	
School Supplies	
School Club(S) Due/Fees	
New Clothing	
Allowances	
Other Living Expenses	

Total Lilving Expenses:_____

February _____

Monthly Expenses

Pet Expenses

Pet Expenses	
Pet Food	
Veterinary Appointments	
New Toys / Treats	
Pet Sitter / Daycare	
Other Pet Expenses	

Total Pet Expenses:

Transportation

Automobile Insurance	
Automobile Payments	
Monthly Fuel Costs	
Repairs / Maintenance	
Fares / Tickets / Etc	
Other Transportation Expenses	

Total Transportation:_____

Gift Expenses

Monthly Birthdays	
Monthly Holidays	
Other Gift Expenses	

Total Gift Expenses:_____

Monthly Expenses

Housing Expenses

Renter's / Homeowner's Insurance	
Cleaning Supplies	
Gradening Supplies	
Furnishings	
Laundry / Dry Cleaning	
Home Maintenance / Repairs	
Household Necessities	
Other Housing Expenses	

Total Housing Expenses:

Recreation

Vacation	
Dining Out	
Entertainment	
Social Events	
Other Recreation Expenses	

Total Recreation Expenses:

Savings

Emergency Fund	
Education Fund	
Retirement Fund	

Total Savings: _____

February

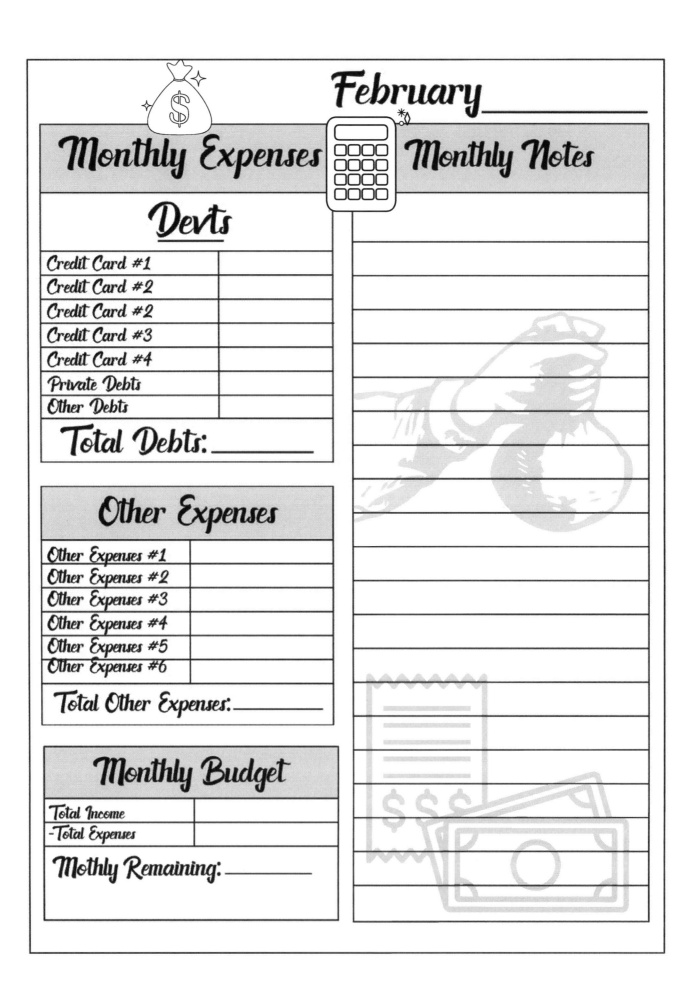

Monthly Expenses

Devts

Credit Card #1	
Credit Card #2	
Credit Card #2	
Credit Card #3	
Credit Card #4	
Private Debts	
Other Debts	

Total Debts: _____

Other Expenses

Other Expenses #1	
Other Expenses #2	
Other Expenses #3	
Other Expenses #4	
Other Expenses #5	
Other Expenses #6	

Total Other Expenses: _____

Monthly Budget

Total Income	
-Total Expenses	

Mothly Remaining: _____

Monthly Notes

Monthly Bill Tracking

Paid	Bill Name	Due Date	Amount Due	Amount Paid	Balance	Payment Method / Notes

Create Your March Budget Here

Monthly Incomes

#	Source	Amount	Date
1			
2			
3			
4			
5			

Total Income:_____

Monthly Expenses

Healthcare

Health Insurance	
Life Insurance	
Dental Insurance	
Doctor Appointment(S)	
Optometry Appointment(S)	
Dental Appointment(S)	
Prescriptions	
Other Medical Expenses	

Total Healthcare:_____

Monthly Expenses (utilities)

Rent/Mortgage	
Electricity Bill	
Water Bill	
Sewage/Trash	
Cabel Bill	
Internet	
Phone Bill(S)	

Total Utilites:_____

notes

Living Expenses

Groceries
Beauty Suplies
Beauty Appointments
Membership Dues/Fees
Daycare/Babysitter
School Supplies
School Club(S) Due/Fees
New Clothing
Allowances
Other Living Expenses

Total Lilving Expenses:_____

March _____

Monthly Expenses

Pet Expenses

Pet Expenses	
Pet Food	
Veterinary Appointments	
New Toys / Treats	
Pet Sitter / Daycare	
Other Pet Expenses	

Total Pet Expenses:

Transportation

Automobile Insurance	
Automobile Payments	
Monthly Fuel Costs	
Repairs / Maintenance	
Fares / Tickets / Etc	
Other Transportation Expenses	

Total Transportation: _____

Gift Expenses

Monthly Birthdays	
Monthly Holidays	
Other Gift Expenses	

Total Gift Expenses: _____

Monthly Expenses

Housing Expenses

Renter's / Homeowner's Insurance	
Cleaning Supplies	
Gardening Supplies	
Furnishings	
Laundry / Dry Cleaning	
Home Maintenance / Repairs	
Household Necessities	
Other Housing Expenses	

Total Housing Expenses:

Recreation

Vacation	
Dining Out	
Entertainment	
Social Events	
Other Recreation Expenses	

Total Recreation Expenses:

Savings

Emergency Fund	
Education Fund	
Retirement Fund	

Total Savings: _____

March _____

Monthly Expenses

Devts

Credit Card #1	
Credit Card #2	
Credit Card #2	
Credit Card #3	
Credit Card #4	
Private Debts	
Other Debts	

Total Debts: _____

Other Expenses

Other Expenses #1	
Other Expenses #2	
Other Expenses #3	
Other Expenses #4	
Other Expenses #5	
Other Expenses #6	

Total Other Expenses: _____

Monthly Budget

Total Income	
-Total Expenses	

Mothly Remaining: _____

Monthly Notes

Monthly Bill Tracking

Paid	Bill Name	Due Date	Amount Due	Amound Paid	Balance	Payment Method / Notes

Create Your April Budget Here

Monthly Incomes

#	Source	Amount	Date
1			
2			
3			
4			
5			

Total Income:_____

Monthly Expenses

Healthcare

Health Insurance	
Life Insurance	
Dental Insurance	
Doctor Appointment(S)	
Optometry Appointment(S)	
Dental Appointment(S)	
Prescriptions	
Other Medical Expenses	

Total Healthcare:_____

Monthly Expenses (utilities)

Rent/Mortgage	
Electricity Bill	
Water Bill	
Sewage/Trash	
Cabel Bill	
Internet	
Phone Bill(S)	

Total Utilites:_____

notes

Living Expenses

Groceries
Beauty Suplies
Beauty Appointments
Membership Dues/Fees
Daycare/Babysitter
School Supplies
School Club(S) Due/Fees
New Clothing
Allowances
Other Living Expenses

Total Lilving Expenses:_____

April _____

Monthly Expenses

Pet Expenses

Pet Expenses	
Pet Food	
Veterinary Appointments	
New Toys / Treats	
Pet Sitter / Daycare	
Other Pet Expenses	

Total Pet Expenses:

Transportation

Automobile Insurance	
Automobile Payments	
Monthly Fuel Costs	
Repairs / Maintenance	
Fares / Tickets / Etc	
Other Transportation Expenses	

Total Transportation:_____

Gift Expenses

Monthly Birthdays	
Monthly Holidays	
Other Gift Expenses	

Total Gift Expenses:_____

Monthly Expenses

Housing Expenses

Renter's / Homeowner's Insurance	
Cleaning Supplies	
Gardening Supplies	
Furnishings	
Laundry / Dry Cleaning	
Home Maintenance / Repairs	
Household Necessities	
Other Housing Expenses	

Total Housing Expenses:

Recreation

Vacation	
Dining Out	
Entertainment	
Social Events	
Other Recreation Expenses	

Total Recreation Expenses:

Savings

Emergency Fund	
Education Fund	
Retirement Fund	

Total Savings:_____

April _____

Monthly Expenses

Devts

Credit Card #1	
Credit Card #2	
Credit Card #2	
Credit Card #3	
Credit Card #4	
Private Debts	
Other Debts	

Total Debts: _____

Other Expenses

Other Expenses #1	
Other Expenses #2	
Other Expenses #3	
Other Expenses #4	
Other Expenses #5	
Other Expenses #6	

Total Other Expenses: _____

Monthly Budget

Total Income	
-Total Expenses	

Mothly Remaining: _____

Monthly Notes

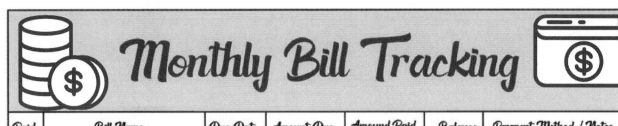

Monthly Bill Tracking

Paid	Bill Name	Due Date	Amount Due	Amound Paid	Balance	Payment Method / Notes

Create Your May Budget Here

Monthly Incomes

#	Source	Amount	Date
1			
2			
3			
4			
5			

Total Income: _____

Monthly Expenses

Healthcare

Health Insurance	
Life Insurance	
Dental Insurance	
Doctor Appointment(S)	
Optometry Appointment(S)	
Dental Appointment(S)	
Prescriptions	
Other Medical Expenses	

Total Healthcare: _____

Monthly Expenses (utilities)

Rent/Mortgage	
Electricity Bill	
Water Bill	
Sewage/Trash	
Cabel Bill	
Internet	
Phone Bill(S)	

Total Utilites: _____

notes

Living Expenses

Groceries	
Beauty Suplies	
Beauty Appointments	
Membership Dues/Fees	
Daycare/Babysitter	
School Supplies	
School Club(S) Due/Fees	
New Clothing	
Allowances	
Other Living Expenses	

Total Lilving Expenses: _____

May_____

Monthly Expenses

Pet Expenses

Pet Expenses	
Pet Food	
Veterinary Appointments	
New Toys / Treats	
Pet Sitter / Daycare	
Other Pet Expenses	

Total Pet Expenses:

Transportation

Automobile Insurance	
Automobile Payments	
Monthly Fuel Costs	
Repairs / Maintenance	
Fares / Tickets / Etc	
Other Transportation Expenses	

Total Transportation:_____

Gift Expenses

Monthly Birthdays	
Monthly Holidays	
Other Gift Expenses	

Total Gift Expenses:_____

Monthly Expenses

Housing Expenses

Renter's / Homeowner's Insurance	
Cleaning Supplies	
Gradening Supplies	
Furnishings	
Laundry / Dry Cleaning	
Home Maintenance / Repairs	
Household Necessities	
Other Housing Expenses	

Total Housing Expenses:

Recreation

Vacation	
Dining Out	
Entertainment	
Social Events	
Other Recreation Expenses	

Total Recreation Expenses:

Savings

Emergency Fund	
Education Fund	
Retirement Fund	

Total Savings:_____

$

May _____

Monthly Expenses

Devts

Credit Card #1	
Credit Card #2	
Credit Card #2	
Credit Card #3	
Credit Card #4	
Private Debts	
Other Debts	

Total Debts: _____

Other Expenses

Other Expenses #1	
Other Expenses #2	
Other Expenses #3	
Other Expenses #4	
Other Expenses #5	
Other Expenses #6	

Total Other Expenses: _____

Monthly Budget

Total Income	
-Total Expenses	

Mothly Remaining: _____

Monthly Notes

Monthly Bill Tracking

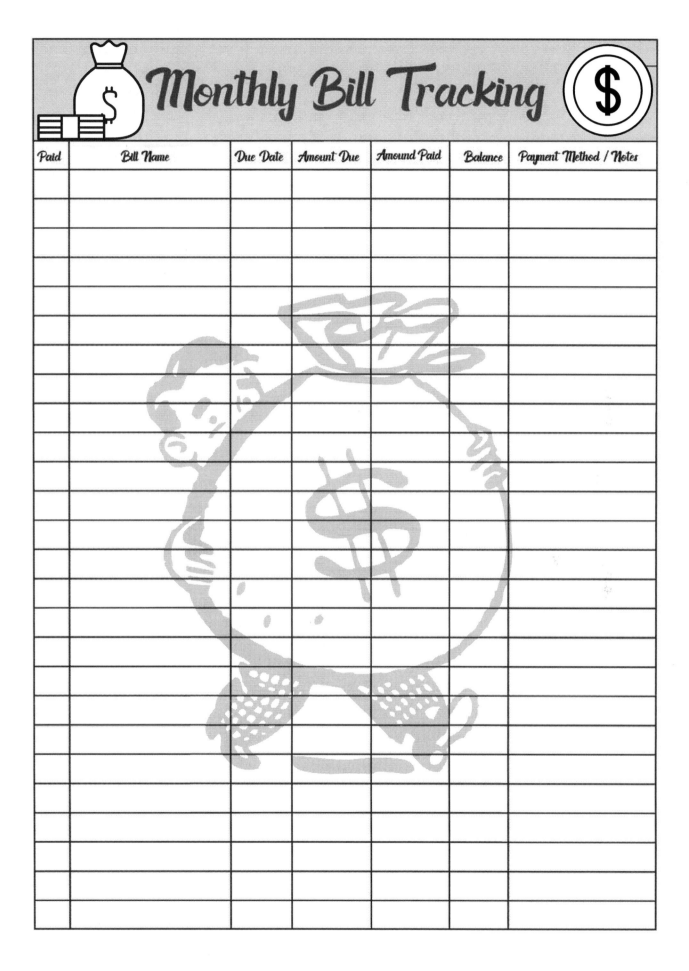

Paid	Bill Name	Due Date	Amount Due	Amound Paid	Balance	Payment Method / Notes

Create Your June Budget Here

Monthly Incomes

#	Source	Amount	Date
1			
2			
3			
4			
5			

Total Income:_____

Monthly Expenses

Healthcare

Health Insurance	
Life Insurance	
Dental Insurance	
Doctor Appointment(S)	
Optometry Appointment(S)	
Dental Appointment(S)	
Prescriptions	
Other Medical Expenses	

Total Healthcare:_____

Monthly Expenses (utilities)

Rent/Mortgage	
Electricity Bill	
Water Bill	
Sewage/Trash	
Cabel Bill	
Internet	
Phone Bill(S)	

Total Utilites:_____

notes

Living Expenses

Groceries	
Beauty Suplies	
Beauty Appointments	
Membership Dues/Fees	
Daycare/Babysitter	
School Supplies	
School Club(S) Due/Fees	
New Clothing	
Allowances	
Other Living Expenses	

Total Lilving Expenses:_____

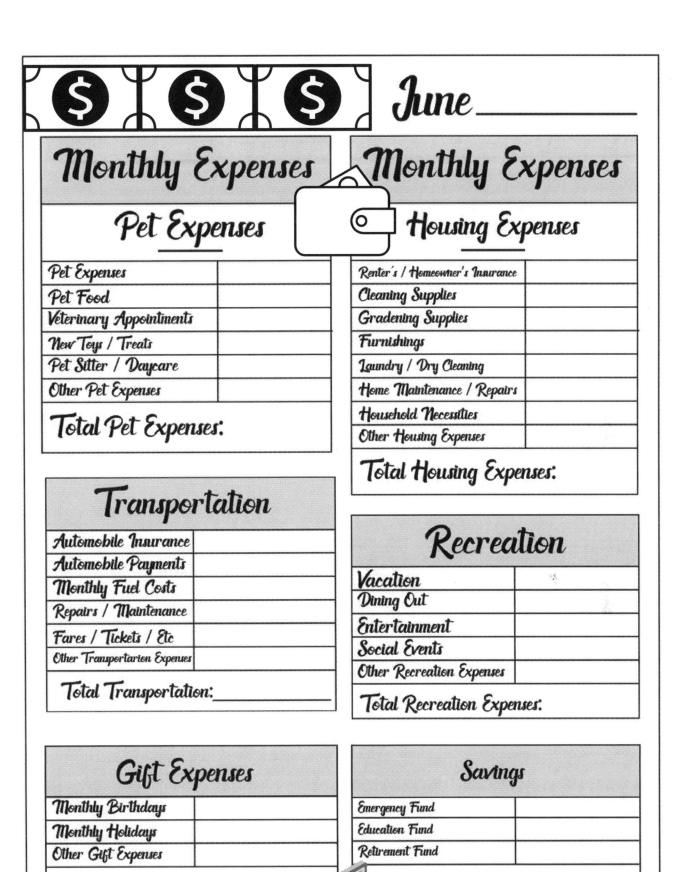

June

Monthly Expenses

Pet Expenses

Pet Expenses	
Pet Food	
Veterinary Appointments	
New Toys / Treats	
Pet Sitter / Daycare	
Other Pet Expenses	

Total Pet Expenses:

Transportation

Automobile Insurance	
Automobile Payments	
Monthly Fuel Costs	
Repairs / Maintenance	
Fares / Tickets / Etc	
Other Transportation Expenses	

Total Transportation:_____

Gift Expenses

Monthly Birthdays	
Monthly Holidays	
Other Gift Expenses	

Total Gift Expenses:_____

Monthly Expenses

Housing Expenses

Renter's / Homeowner's Insurance	
Cleaning Supplies	
Gradening Supplies	
Furnishings	
Laundry / Dry Cleaning	
Home Maintenance / Repairs	
Household Necessities	
Other Housing Expenses	

Total Housing Expenses:

Recreation

Vacation	
Dining Out	
Entertainment	
Social Events	
Other Recreation Expenses	

Total Recreation Expenses:

Savings

Emergency Fund	
Education Fund	
Retirement Fund	

Total Savings:_____

June _____

Monthly Expenses

Devts

Credit Card #1	
Credit Card #2	
Credit Card #2	
Credit Card #3	
Credit Card #4	
Private Debts	
Other Debts	

Total Debts: _____

Other Expenses

Other Expenses #1	
Other Expenses #2	
Other Expenses #3	
Other Expenses #4	
Other Expenses #5	
Other Expenses #6	

Total Other Expenses: _____

Monthly Budget

Total Income	
-Total Expenses	

Mothly Remaining: _____

Monthly Notes

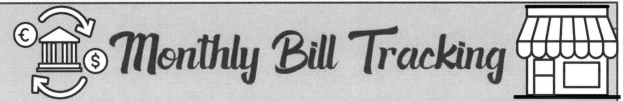

Monthly Bill Tracking

Paid	Bill Name	Due Date	Amount Due	Amount Paid	Balance	Payment Method / Notes

Create Your July Budget Here

Monthly Incomes

#	Source	Amount	Date
1			
2			
3			
4			
5			

Total Income: _____

Monthly Expenses

Healthcare

Health Insurance	
Life Insurance	
Dental Insurance	
Doctor Appointment(S)	
Optometry Appointment(S)	
Dental Appointment(S)	
Prescriptions	
Other Medical Expenses	

Total Healthcare: _____

Monthly Expenses (utilities)

Rent/Mortgage	
Electricity Bill	
Water Bill	
Sewage/Trash	
Cabel Bill	
Internet	
Phone Bill(S)	

Total Utilites: _____

notes

Living Expenses

Groceries
Beauty Suplies
Beauty Appointments
Membership Dues/Fees
Daycare/Babysitter
School Supplies
School Club(S) Due/Fees
New Clothing
Allowances
Other Living Expenses

Total Lilving Expenses: _____

July _____

Monthly Expenses

Pet Expenses

Pet Expenses	
Pet Food	
Veterinary Appointments	
New Toys / Treats	
Pet Sitter / Daycare	
Other Pet Expenses	

Total Pet Expenses:

Transportation

Automobile Insurance	
Automobile Payments	
Monthly Fuel Costs	
Repairs / Maintenance	
Fares / Tickets / Etc	
Other Transportation Expenses	

Total Transportation:_____

Gift Expenses

Monthly Birthdays	
Monthly Holidays	
Other Gift Expenses	

Total Gift Expenses:_____

Monthly Expenses

Housing Expenses

Renter's / Homeowner's Insurance	
Cleaning Supplies	
Gradening Supplies	
Furnishings	
Laundry / Dry Cleaning	
Home Maintenance / Repairs	
Household Necessities	
Other Housing Expenses	

Total Housing Expenses:

Recreation

Vacation	
Dining Out	
Entertainment	
Social Events	
Other Recreation Expenses	

Total Recreation Expenses:

Savings

Emergency Fund	
Education Fund	
Retirement Fund	

Total Savings:_____

July _____

Monthly Expenses

Devts

Credit Card #1	
Credit Card #2	
Credit Card #2	
Credit Card #3	
Credit Card #4	
Private Debts	
Other Debts	

Total Debts: _____

Other Expenses

Other Expenses #1	
Other Expenses #2	
Other Expenses #3	
Other Expenses #4	
Other Expenses #5	
Other Expenses #6	

Total Other Expenses: _____

Monthly Budget

Total Income	
-Total Expenses	

Mothly Remaining: _____

Monthly Notes

Monthly Bill Tracking

Paid	Bill Name	Due Date	Amount Due	Amound Paid	Balance	Payment Method / Notes

% ✓ Create Your August Budget Here % ✓

Monthly Incomes

#	Source	Amount	Date
1			
2			
3			
4			
5			

Total Income: _____

Monthly Expenses

Healthcare

Health Insurance	
Life Insurance	
Dental Insurance	
Doctor Appointment(S)	
Optometry Appointment(S)	
Dental Appointment(S)	
Prescriptions	
Other Medical Expenses	

Total Healthcare: _____

Monthly Expenses (utilities)

Rent/Mortgage	
Electricity Bill	
Water Bill	
Sewage/Trash	
Cabel Bill	
Internet	
Phone Bill(S)	

Total Utilites: _____

notes

Living Expenses

Groceries
Beauty Suplies
Beauty Appointments
Membership Dues/Fees
Daycare/Babysitter
School Supplies
School Club(S) Due/Fees
New Clothing
Allowances
Other Living Expenses

Total Lilving Expenses: _____

August _____

Monthly Expenses

Pet Expenses

Pet Expenses	
Pet Food	
Veterinary Appointments	
New Toys / Treats	
Pet Sitter / Daycare	
Other Pet Expenses	

Total Pet Expenses:

Transportation

Automobile Insurance	
Automobile Payments	
Monthly Fuel Costs	
Repairs / Maintenance	
Fares / Tickets / Etc	
Other Transportation Expenses	

Total Transportation: _____

Gift Expenses

Monthly Birthdays	
Monthly Holidays	
Other Gift Expenses	

Total Gift Expenses: _____

Monthly Expenses

Housing Expenses

Renter's / Homeowner's Insurance	
Cleaning Supplies	
Gardening Supplies	
Furnishings	
Laundry / Dry Cleaning	
Home Maintenance / Repairs	
Household Necessities	
Other Housing Expenses	

Total Housing Expenses:

Recreation

Vacation	
Dining Out	
Entertainment	
Social Events	
Other Recreation Expenses	

Total Recreation Expenses:

Savings

Emergency Fund	
Education Fund	
Retirement Fund	

Total Savings: _____

August _____

Monthly Expenses

Devts

Credit Card #1	
Credit Card #2	
Credit Card #2	
Credit Card #3	
Credit Card #4	
Private Debts	
Other Debts	

Total Debts: _____

Other Expenses

Other Expenses #1	
Other Expenses #2	
Other Expenses #3	
Other Expenses #4	
Other Expenses #5	
Other Expenses #6	

Total Other Expenses: _____

Monthly Budget

Total Income	
-Total Expenses	

Mothly Remaining: _____

Monthly Notes

Monthly Bill Tracking

Paid	Bill Name	Due Date	Amount Due	Amount Paid	Balance	Payment Method / Notes

Create Your September Budget Here

Monthly Incomes

#	Source	Amount	Date
1			
2			
3			
4			
5			

Total Income: _____

Monthly Expenses

Healthcare

Health Insurance	
Life Insurance	
Dental Insurance	
Doctor Appointment(S)	
Optometry Appointment(S)	
Dental Appointment(S)	
Prescriptions	
Other Medical Expenses	

Total Healthcare: _____

Monthly Expenses (utilities)

Rent/Mortgage	
Electricity Bill	
Water Bill	
Sewage/Trash	
Cabel Bill	
Internet	
Phone Bill(S)	

Total Utilites: _____

notes

Living Expenses

Groceries
Beauty Suplies
Beauty Appointments
Membership Dues/Fees
Daycare/Babysitter
School Supplies
School Club(S) Due/Fees
New Clothing
Allowances
Other Living Expenses

Total Lilving Expenses: _____

September_____

Monthly Expenses

Pet Expenses

Pet Expenses	
Pet Food	
Veterinary Appointments	
New Toys / Treats	
Pet Sitter / Daycare	
Other Pet Expenses	

Total Pet Expenses:

Transportation

Automobile Insurance	
Automobile Payments	
Monthly Fuel Costs	
Repairs / Maintenance	
Fares / Tickets / Etc	
Other Transportation Expenses	

Total Transportation:_____

Gift Expenses

Monthly Birthdays	
Monthly Holidays	
Other Gift Expenses	

Total Gift Expenses:_____

Monthly Expenses

Housing Expenses

Renter's / Homeowner's Insurance	
Cleaning Supplies	
Gradening Supplies	
Furnishings	
Laundry / Dry Cleaning	
Home Maintenance / Repairs	
Household Necessities	
Other Housing Expenses	

Total Housing Expenses:

Recreation

Vacation	
Dining Out	
Entertainment	
Social Events	
Other Recreation Expenses	

Total Recreation Expenses:

Savings

Emergency Fund	
Education Fund	
Retirement Fund	

Total Savings:_____

September_____

Monthly Expenses

Devts

Credit Card #1	
Credit Card #2	
Credit Card #2	
Credit Card #3	
Credit Card #4	
Private Debts	
Other Debts	

Total Debts:_____

Other Expenses

Other Expenses #1	
Other Expenses #2	
Other Expenses #3	
Other Expenses #4	
Other Expenses #5	
Other Expenses #6	

Total Other Expenses:_____

Monthly Budget

Total Income	
-Total Expenses	

Mothly Remaining:_____

Monthly Notes

 # Monthly Bill Tracking

Paid	Bill Name	Due Date	Amount Due	Amount Paid	Balance	Payment Method / Notes

Create Your October Budget Here

Monthly Incomes

#	Source	Amount	Date
1			
2			
3			
4			
5			

Total Income:_____

Monthly Expenses

Healthcare

Health Insurance	
Life Insurance	
Dental Insurance	
Doctor Appointment(S)	
Optometry Appointment(S)	
Dental Appointment(S)	
Prescriptions	
Other Medical Expenses	

Total Healthcare:_____

Monthly Expenses (utilities)

Rent/Mortgage	
Electricity Bill	
Water Bill	
Sewage/Trash	
Cabel Bill	
Internet	
Phone Bill(S)	

Total Utilites:_____

notes

Living Expenses

Groceries
Beauty Suplies
Beauty Appointments
Membership Dues/Fees
Daycare/Babysitter
School Supplies
School Club(S) Due/Fees
New Clothing
Allowances
Other Living Expenses

Total Lilving Expenses:_____

October _____

Monthly Expenses

Pet Expenses

Pet Expenses	
Pet Food	
Veterinary Appointments	
New Toys / Treats	
Pet Sitter / Daycare	
Other Pet Expenses	

Total Pet Expenses:

Monthly Expenses

Housing Expenses

Renter's / Homeowner's Insurance	
Cleaning Supplies	
Gradening Supplies	
Furnishings	
Laundry / Dry Cleaning	
Home Maintenance / Repairs	
Household Necessities	
Other Housing Expenses	

Total Housing Expenses:

Transportation

Automobile Insurance	
Automobile Payments	
Monthly Fuel Costs	
Repairs / Maintenance	
Fares / Tickets / Etc	
Other Transportarion Expenses	

Total Transportation:_____

Recreation

Vacation	
Dining Out	
Entertainment	
Social Events	
Other Recreation Expenses	

Total Recreation Expenses:

Gift Expenses

Monthly Birthdays	
Monthly Holidays	
Other Gift Expenses	

Total Gift Expenses:_____

Savings

Emergency Fund	
Education Fund	
Retirement Fund	

Total Savings:_____

$ € £ October _____

Monthly Expenses

Devts

Credit Card #1	
Credit Card #2	
Credit Card #2	
Credit Card #3	
Credit Card #4	
Private Debts	
Other Debts	

Total Debts: _____

Other Expenses

Other Expenses #1	
Other Expenses #2	
Other Expenses #3	
Other Expenses #4	
Other Expenses #5	
Other Expenses #6	

Total Other Expenses: _____

Monthly Budget

Total Income	
-Total Expenses	

Mothly Remaining: _____

Monthly Notes

 # Monthly Bill Tracking

Paid	Bill Name	Due Date	Amount Due	Amount Paid	Balance	Payment Method / Notes

Create Your November Budget Here

Monthly Incomes

#	Source	Amount	Date
1			
2			
3			
4			
5			

Total Income: _____

Monthly Expenses

Healthcare

Health Insurance	
Life Insurance	
Dental Insurance	
Doctor Appointment(S)	
Optometry Appointment(S)	
Dental Appointment(S)	
Prescriptions	
Other Medical Expenses	

Total Healthcare: _____

Monthly Expenses (utilities)

Rent/Mortgage	
Electricity Bill	
Water Bill	
Sewage/Trash	
Cabel Bill	
Internet	
Phone Bill(S)	

Total Utilites: _____

notes

Living Expenses

Groceries
Beauty Suplies
Beauty Appointments
Membership Dues/Fees
Daycare/Babysitter
School Supplies
School Club(S) Due/Fees
New Clothing
Allowances
Other Living Expenses

Total Lilving Expenses: _____

Novemver _____

Monthly Expenses

Pet Expenses

Pet Expenses	
Pet Food	
Veterinary Appointments	
New Toys / Treats	
Pet Sitter / Daycare	
Other Pet Expenses	

Total Pet Expenses:

Transportation

Automobile Insurance	
Automobile Payments	
Monthly Fuel Costs	
Repairs / Maintenance	
Fares / Tickets / Etc	
Other Transportation Expenses	

Total Transportation: _____

Gift Expenses

Monthly Birthdays	
Monthly Holidays	
Other Gift Expenses	

Total Gift Expenses: _____

Monthly Expenses

Housing Expenses

Renter's / Homeowner's Insurance	
Cleaning Supplies	
Gradening Supplies	
Furnishings	
Laundry / Dry Cleaning	
Home Maintenance / Repairs	
Household Necessities	
Other Housing Expenses	

Total Housing Expenses:

Recreation

Vacation	
Dining Out	
Entertainment	
Social Events	
Other Recreation Expenses	

Total Recreation Expenses:

Savings

Emergency Fund	
Education Fund	
Retirement Fund	

Total Savings: _____

Novemver

Monthly Expenses

Devts

Credit Card #1	
Credit Card #2	
Credit Card #2	
Credit Card #3	
Credit Card #4	
Private Debts	
Other Debts	

Total Debts: _____

Other Expenses

Other Expenses #1	
Other Expenses #2	
Other Expenses #3	
Other Expenses #4	
Other Expenses #5	
Other Expenses #6	

Total Other Expenses: _____

Monthly Budget

Total Income	
-Total Expenses	

Mothly Remaining: _____

Monthly Notes

Monthly Bill Tracking

Paid	Bill Name	Due Date	Amount Due	Amount Paid	Balance	Payment Method / Notes

Create Your December Budget Here

Monthly Incomes

#	Source	Amount	Date
1			
2			
3			
4			
5			

Total Income:_____

Monthly Expenses

Healthcare

Health Insurance	
Life Insurance	
Dental Insurance	
Doctor Appointiment(S)	
Optometry Appointiment(S)	
Dental Appointiment(S)	
Prescriptions	
Other Medical Expenses	

Total Healthcare:_____

Monthly Expenses (utilities)

Rent/Mortgage	
Electricity Bill	
Water Bill	
Sewage/Trash	
Cabel Bill	
Internet	
Phone Bill(S)	

Total Utilites:_____

notes

Living Expenses

Groceries
Beauty Suplies
Beauty Appointments
Membership Dues/Fees
Daycare/Babysitter
School Supplies
School Club(S) Due/Fees
New Clothing
Allowances
Other Living Expenses

Total Lilving Expenses:_____

December_____

Monthly Expenses

Pet Expenses

Pet Expenses	
Pet Food	
Veterinary Appointments	
New Toys / Treats	
Pet Sitter / Daycare	
Other Pet Expenses	

Total Pet Expenses:

Transportation

Automobile Insurance	
Automobile Payments	
Monthly Fuel Costs	
Repairs / Maintenance	
Fares / Tickets / Etc	
Other Transportation Expenses	

Total Transportation:_____

Gift Expenses

Monthly Birthdays	
Monthly Holidays	
Other Gift Expenses	

Total Gift Expenses:_____

Monthly Expenses

Housing Expenses

Renter's / Homeowner's Insurance	
Cleaning Supplies	
Gradening Supplies	
Furnishings	
Laundry / Dry Cleaning	
Home Maintenance / Repairs	
Household Necessities	
Other Housing Expenses	

Total Housing Expenses:

Recreation

Vacation	
Dining Out	
Entertainment	
Social Events	
Other Recreation Expenses	

Total Recreation Expenses:

Savings

Emergency Fund	
Education Fund	
Retirement Fund	

Total Savings:_____

December

Monthly Expenses

Devts

Credit Card #1	
Credit Card #2	
Credit Card #2	
Credit Card #3	
Credit Card #4	
Private Debts	
Other Debts	

Total Debts: _____

Other Expenses

Other Expenses #1	
Other Expenses #2	
Other Expenses #3	
Other Expenses #4	
Other Expenses #5	
Other Expenses #6	

Total Other Expenses: _____

Monthly Budget

Total Income	
-Total Expenses	

Mothly Remaining: _____

Monthly Notes

Monthly Bill Tracking

Paid	Bill Name	Due Date	Amount Due	Amount Paid	Balance	Payment Method / Notes

Thank you!

We hope you enjoyed our book.

As a small family company, your feedback is very important to us.
Please let us know how you like our book at:
jami.jamesson.j@gmail.com

* These books come in several designs to suit your unique taste.
Please check the author's profile (**Jami Jamesson**) for more designs.

* Your comments are greatly appreciated!

* We also highly recommend visiting the following author pages where
you will find books for the children in your life by **Alis Nicole Uson**
and fashion / makeup / nail art by **Jimi Jamesson**.

Thank you and have a wonderful year!

Made in the USA
Monee, IL
11 January 2022

88664949R00057